T0208585

The HOLY CRY

Lillie Mae Hipps-Dickerson

BALBOA.
PRESS
A DIVISION OF HAY HOUSE

Balboa Press books may be ordered through booksellers or by contacting:

Balboa Press
A Division of Hay House
1663 Liberty Drive
Bloomington, IN 47403
www.balboapress.com
1 (877) 407-4847

Because of the dynamic nature of the Internet, any web addresses or links contained in this book may have changed since publication and may no longer be valid. The views expressed in this work are solely those of the author and do not necessarily reflect the views of the publisher, and the publisher hereby disclaims any responsibility for them.

The author of this book does not dispense medical advice or prescribe the use of any technique as a form of treatment for physical, emotional, or medical problems without the advice of a physician, either directly or indirectly. The intent of the author is only to offer information of a general nature to help you in your quest for emotional and spiritual well-being. In the event you use any of the information in this book for yourself, which is your constitutional right, the author and the publisher assume no responsibility for your actions.

Any people depicted in stock imagery provided by Getty Images are models, and such images are being used for illustrative purposes only. Certain stock imagery © Getty Images.

Scripture taken from the King James Version of the Bible.

Print information available on the last page.

ISBN: 978-1-9822-3579-6 (sc)
ISBN: 978-1-9822-3580-2 (e)

Balboa Press rev. date: 09/27/2019

Table of Contents

1

A HOLY WOMAN

Gigi had respect for the Lord spirit as she came with
A white rose in her hand so she can be blessing by the
Holy power in prayer. Cain saw a miracle in the sky that
Came up from the field of life
A little flock of birds bare the holy faith in a tiny moment
Of peace so he could be a blessing to someone in the
Precious land with holiness that rose up from the ground
To show the Lord your salvation in the dry land of prayer
Gigi came out of the gate to go the temple and praise the
Congregation of Grace so they respect the holy power
In the mouth of the living God because he could never leave
Her a long in time of sad time in her life
Her life is impossible on the battle field of peace
                Psalm 29 (11) KJV
Cain saw a tiny light in a star shine around the world for a
Christmas blessing.
When he came home from his date and he found his father
On the floor because he had a heart attack and his mother was
In the living room so their call for an ambulance to right away
Because her husband was had a heart attack
Hope rode in the ambulance with Ray

2

CAIN DROVE TO THE HOSPITAL WITH HIS SISTER DOLLIE

Hope was cry when her children reach the hospital
Because Ray was very sick, and he stay in the hospital
For two weeds
His church prayed for him on Sunday morning
Rev Lower and some of the congregation went to the
Hospital to visit him
Mile was a very good friend of Cain for about ten
Years and their meet in art class and Mile Family
To the city about twenty years go
Cherry Lee Down worship at the holiness Church
When she ran into Mile one Sunday at church and she
Was very happy to see him because they not talk or
Seen one other for a long time
She was head up a gospel shop for member joint
The choir
Ray could not work any more
He and Hope were very happy with their life
Cain were plan a secret vacation for Dollie with the
Doctor. They went to Believed Town for two weeks
To enjoy them self and DR Heart was single
DR Heart and Cain was friend for a long time
The friend had a good time in Believed Town
And they went to church to visit one Sunday
They shop and have a good time on they vacation
In Joy City when their meet Bishop Wait and he show
Them around the city.
Cain and Dollie depart for home the next morning and
Their labor was in the spirit of the Lord wisdom and

3

THEY LOVE WAS GROWN BY FAITH IN THEIR HEART.

Mile was appointed to another church in Among
Prayer Town and testify of their journey of Blameless
To be building in the spirit of the poor whom need
Help in their life with joy
The congregation welcome them back home with a
Peace offering that came for them in the church that
Prevail in their life with a moment of laying close to
One of other in the spirit of the Lord hope in prayer
                    For everyone
The increase of faith that came out of your heart
Into the congregation in love that went up into the
Kingdom of the holy church
Canny was a bishop in the holy land of God kingdom
And he promised to be faithful in the church of judgment
When his life came in the steward ship of grace to be
Hold in the spirit of teacher in the wilderness
His will was to do good in the present on the Lord
And the congregation and his family were very important
To him in love and he prayed for them
Mile went to town to shop for a gift and when he entered
Into the mall to meet with an old friend of his and this
Was a great time for them to visiting because they have not
Seen each other for about six years.
Law have become a doctor and move away he came to visit
With his mother because his father had died three weeks
Earlier
Law was marriage to Branch and they have a new baby girl
Eve Ann and she was a blessing to them

4

A MESSENGER CAME RUNNING
INTO THE CHURCH

to tell the congregation that someone had
Been killing down the road and he was come this way
to the church with the gun in his hand and the angels
was watch over the church and someone call the
police to come right away and their lock the church
door and their have good time talking and sing for two
hours so the congregation have a grand old time
singing hymns and Rev Word order lunch for the church
whom stay at church and Rev Word wife Olivia and the
children went into fellowship hall to play games in the
spirit of the Lord and the dark side of the kill rose up at
the door of the church and came in to kneel and
pray for mercy because the blood was on his hand with a
powerful spirit that enter Harry heart with a cry for
Rev word to blessing him before the police come to
Arresting him. He went down to the offer flood in
Peace to pray for mercy and in half hour time late
The church was lock and everyone went home
Lee and Rain walk around the park because they
Was in a total shock
Harry proclaim his life after the killing a stranger
After broke into his house he learned a valuable lesson
In God faith for the world and he learn how to love
His self in the precious spirit of the Holy Ghost
He spent ten years in prison when he got out
The Lord restore his love for the church back to him
In the holy spirit and Gigi was draw close to the chief
On the battle field when Rain approach the wilderness

5

IN THE PRAY LINE OF HOLINESS

Some of the congregation welcome Harry into the church
With a soft word in their soul for him to be servant of the
Lord
Lee return to his home church the next month in Peace
Worship Town to visit his mother Silver Ann. Mile came to
Meet his friend at the park to bring freedom into the world
And under the shadow of his faith in due time of wisdom
That came down on a rainbow in a moment of praise when
Teo of the shepherd follow the church toward the worship hill
In the vineyard of wisdom. The Lord spread out a net for every
One to fall into with their life in holiness as they watch over
Their mouth in the holy power of victory
Silver Ann came into the spirit and went into the pond of life
To inform the congregation that she would be go to be
Speak at Fire Church on next Sunday morning I was listed to
The Grace in the precious word of the Holy Ghost and I fine a
Place to go out into the vineyard to pray in victory and I will fear
Not the Lord by his power as I enter the church with the little
Angels that came and bow down at the cross
My ministry are strong in my heart among my friends that are
Standing on the battle field of freedom when I poured out my
Heart into a tiny vessel of happiness that pass into the open air
My life is close to the Lord in time of faith that shall carry you
In his holiness of victory from day to day with your grace that
Flow upon the heart in justified moment in the pure blood of love
In salvation that walk among the vineyard in prayer
Mile said of his precious blood running down from the cross into
A river glory with honor that creature in the host of heaven when he

6

RECEIVE THE POWER FROM THE LORD PRAISE IN WORSHIP OF THE CHURCH

Because his mother was holy in the eye of the Lord and he cast out
A little word of holiness in the presence of Rev Word to proceed
In the issue of a clean spirit with the angels according to his be loving
Father in heaven
Cain prayer with his church in victory of faith for the whole congregation
For peace because the Lord draw him close to the holy cross in his
season
Was a time for his to become heal and he stretched out his life in a
moment
Of grace for the Lord holiness in wisdom
Someday I shall stand up in the holy line of freedom to be judge by
the faith
In the air with the angels and one day he went out to the school and set
Down with the children to talk with them because their life is in the
Lord
Victory and my soul are not forsake by the hand of the Lord
Gigi had a happy visit with her family in the hospital because she has
cancer
And was heal by the power of the Lord faith in her heart.
After five months she consumed her dream in the gospel field in a
blessing
The command of the church was great in the Holy Spirit. She met a
little
Girl whom was name Daily Angel Fire. Gigi came close to Daily and
her
Family did not attend church in the Change Town where their live
The little girl learned to love the church at the age of sixteen and she
move

Close into the spirit of the Lord nobody to judge her in the hard time of

Peace that came upon her in due time of righteousness season and her mother

Start go to church and joint the choir and the family was blessing by the

Prayer meekness in the spirit of time

One Sunday the hold family went to the service at church and the Lord delivered

Her father from drugs and Law committed his life to Lord and he became a deacon

Law honor his blessing in the Lord and he was strong man in the gospel of the

Church to hear a word from the Lord and in his life was victory that came out

7

OF THE ANSWERING OF HIS FAITH IN THE WHIRLWIND OF THE POWER THAT

Art pour out his soul when the angels into the open spirit of paradise
That flow to someone heart with a tiny piece of their life in a vessel
Of praise
Harry came to preacher to the lost soul in the wilderness of
Salvation in the worship service to bring peoples close to the
Lord after Sunday service he went to visit the hospital and when
He ran into old friend of his
Cherry Lee was very happy to see him because it was about three
Years since their seen one other and they visit was amaze to her
Mother and the holy spirit fall into a praise dance of grace for both
Of them
Their hug for a long time after Harry left her that afternoon he and hope
To see her again in the future
All the holy women came together in a moment of victory to pray
for peace in the church for the tiny baby in **Bethlehem**
the preacher dance on the cross of salvation in never the less praise
to the congregation that leaden them into a battle of holiness
my grace are a point of judgment in my life as I march into the
vineyard with the gospel saint on the battle field of wisdom
Cherry Lee was happy in the holy spirit of righteousness because
She was blind by her faith in the Lord garden of pure rose when
She heard a soft voice that came down in the season of love due
In time of a prison to come clean by the open hand of a shepherd
In high power that dwell in midst of someone heart that burn in
Hope according to their soul in the Holy City of Holiness when the
Shepherd came out of the field with a little child in his arms of
Prayer in a word from heaven
One moment my glory is consumed upon a shine star that

8

LEADEN TO THE CROSS. I CONTACT
ALL THE ANGELS IN THE

Vineyard of the prison to come and dance in the spirit
Of the Lord because the women were fill with praise
In their voice when the Lord came into a tiny cup of oil
To clean they life in the shaken wind with prayer
One day God sent down a messenger for the church in
The wilderness to come and be bless by his holy hands
Of praise. Cain was amaze by the dance of the young
Children that came in off the street to sing for the Lord
Their cast out a unquenchable faith to rise out of heaven
In a peace offering for someone to be safe by the power
In their heart with a moment of holiness
Cherry Lee influence them to stay and by bless by the
Holy word in love and one of them wanted to be baptize
By the grace in his soul and Daily said oh my Lord what have
I walk into, my life are full of victory Hank stay there and
Joint the church and his walked out his life after two years
And one Sunday morning Jeep came for a visit three
Month late joint too their have a dream of conform a hymn
To the congregation. Cain was amaze at their voice it touches
His spirit that no one know now
Cherry Lee have a place in her heart for a moment of
Peace to cover her grace in prayer for her family so she
Could see the expected love that the Lord bring into
The soul who are on drug and one day she walked around
Town and gather the peoples on the street to church on
Sunday and one of them came to fine her on a Friday night
Because her life was a mess and wanted to go to church
With her Sunday Ward was happy she came to the Lord

9

BY PRAY IN THE JUDGMENT OF HOLINESS AND HER LIFE WAS A

Blessing to her family and her mother was very glad for
Her
Ward have a dream one night according to the open spirit
She was with the Lord in the temple in his holy word that
Came rushing into her heart and she was off drug for about
Years
Before the Lord called her to become a singing and she hear
His soft voice in her spirit with her faith that came upon a star
Of time
One Saturday morning the church hand out bibles to the
Peoples who want to learn all about the Lord word in love
Daily came in out the street to prepare her life in a way
That touch the young children by the grace among them
As she grown up in the Lord wisdom and her soul was boldness
In the gospel at the age of seven and she started to preacher
The word to the congregation in the young people Church with
Meekness that full someone heart according to the faith in holy
Moment of peace for them to stand up I the gospel to enjoy the
Love that came down from heaven with a touch of victory of that
Approach the Bishop life in the church and all the young children
Song a hymn to the parents in time of salvation that fall from
Someone soul when the Lord came to them in holiness of they
Life in the spirit of paradise. Daily remain in the Holy Town of
Righteousness when a messenger came with everything in
Their hand for a blessing from the Lord for the congregation
of peace and her word was powerful in the holy name of
the Holy Ghost that belong to the saints on the battle
filed in wisdom and one of the young children told they

10

TESTIMONY IN THE CHURCH AND THE FOLLOW THE VERSION OF

Her life in the grace with the Lord faith in her heart.
The young girls grown up and became holy by the hand of God
Freedom for the world
Harry enter the holy land with his judgment of peace to
Become hole in his life to serve the Lord in the prison for his sins
Of wickedness after ten years he got out of prison and married
To holy woman that believer in the church with all Of her heart
He was a shepherd according to his wife in the gospel of his
Religion

11

THE HOLY GLORY IN YOUR SEASON

Bay speak in the salvation as he worshipped in his power due to
The cast in the witness of the precious bible to pay his way through
College by singing at a little club on the weekend and some after
Noon on the outside of town in Give City on the weekend and at noon
And he met Tellie one afternoon in the club
Their attending the same college was their met and start talking

12

ONE NIGHT AND ON SUNDAY MORNING THEIR ATTENDING CHURCH

Together. They friend ship was a free spirit in wisdom
The season was perfect for the angels to come together
With the holy blessing in the church. God sent down a little
That fall into the preacher heart for a word of worship
And my faith came into my soul with a praise offering that
Behold my life with the answered in the open wind of a tiny
Moment of joy for me to be someone in a blessing for the
Lord in a prayer of freedom in music for the congregation
To hear a sound in their soul for the new baby. Jay Zip came
And arranged a hymn for Bay to play in the church of glory
And I will climb this hill with the help of the Lord in my life
With a moment for me to be happy when I walk by his word
In my life and I pray to the Lord for him to cast me a little
Blessing in a time of salvation that I shall stand up in his spirit
Branch was against the sad time in her life and her little
Sister Jet was very happy in the church of Give City. The preacher
Have a command for her from the Lord in a soft voice in praise
That reproach the spirit to respecter your salvation with
The holy pack of wisdom that enter the strong faith with
The Lord believer moment according to your power in pray
And when their mother came home from work with a gift
For the girls
Jet rose up in a free time of her victory to receive her gift
And she rewarded her mother with a little kiss in the spirit of
The Holy ghost with a word that came out of the heart of
Wisdom that flow out of the air into a vessel of meekness
That dance all around the room with a time of happiness and

13

SHE WAITED FOR A WORD FROM THE LORD WITH A WITNESS THAT

was close in fear of her anointed power in the token of your
magnify judgment in grace. A picture came upon her heart
from her father who have die three year ago in a wicked power
on the battle ground in the vineyard
someone followed close behind a shepherd in the Lord holiness
of peace that came near to her spirt in Zion
Dean was injury in the line of fire in the judgment on the battle
Field of peace and he climb upon a mountain of faith for him to
See the salvation in the precious spirit of wisdom that remove
The poor blessing in serve in the Lord wreath that laid on the
Cross in a hero heart of glory and one day I shall honor the
Little lost soul who fall into wicked hand of Satan
I set down at his foot of the holy cross to see the shepherd
In the temple when they pray for peace in the world
Law went upon a hill in victory to talk with the angels for
A witness before the Lord with a tiny burden to be deliver
In time of trouble. He went out into a secret part of
Holiness to walk in his faith before the Lord saints on
The in the vineyard as he stands up for the holy angel in
A strange power of calling into the holy glory
Bay hear a voice in the wind upon a rock for the
Shepherd to stand in peace of thunder and he lift up
His soul for their life in the shining light of judgment
In salvation as they ran to be safe from the wicked spirit
In Satan power
My life was submitted to the Lord congregation in time
Of a blessing to dance in the moment of meekness that rise
Up from the dust of the foundation in the firmament of glory

14

THAT APPEAR BEFORE THE CHURCH WHEN THE HOLY ANGELS

Gather to song a hymn in the shadow of darkness upon
The void of your faith in the church
The sin is a light that shine over the water in your heart
When you come whole in the spirit of spirit with the holy
Testimony that show you up in your life. The Lord came
And receiver me in his happiness of a innocent sight of
Glory and I have a reason to serve him for the bondage
In my faith that he has for me and his spirit in victory
Bay was talk to the congregation after Sunday service
Jet came and minister to the children in the spirit of wisdom
When she saw Dean standing by the mother of the church
To be sacrifice her life back to the Lord with the moment
Of his grace that came into the sound of respect for
The preacher
The Lord sent out his praise for me to dance around a tiny
Christmas tree with a word under my tongue for me to be
Innocent in his precious blood of a miracle that fall into
The church with the Holy Pray so I can receiver my testimony
In his holy name. Someone stripped the break power in Satan
When enter the holy salvation of bandage as the children
Prayer in wisdom of their judgment in peace to the kingdom
Sun was a great woman that came upon a little field in the
Holy City of command her spirit was a offering of respect for
The church and she prepare a tiny bowl of rose for the pastor
As a witness before the congregation when they hear a voice
In their heart when they prayer in the spirit
The sound of a small child was singing a hymn to the Lord in the
Power of victory to become a witness in the salvation of pure

15

MOMENT IN BELIEVED THE JUDGMENT THAT FOLLOW THE SHEPHERD

In the vineyard with praise with her faith as she March into the
Plan of the Lord calling for her life to be happy with a moment
Of joy with the shepherd in the wilderness when they prayer
For a little peace in the spirit and one of the little children was cry
Out in salvation of holiness as a witness to the Lord
My tongue shall speak in the innocent blood of a blessing for you
To become whole by his grace in his precious name
One day I shall reach out to the church when I gather all the
Shepherd in the vineyard of Freedom and my faith went up in
The sight of the Lord when Sun start to perform a praise dance
With the teams in the church and her soul was not in the bottom
Hole of the glory offering in a type on his victory and Law show up
In God faith of someone life that was not easy for them in the
Power with the Lord delighted in the holy word of his glory
Your season are a big part of the beginning in your life as you walk
In the path that are before you in the present of your blessing in
His glory with a moment in your believer in prayer faith of the
Holy church when the Lord open your heart for you to be at
Peace with yourself and love the world with a position attitude
In your season of heaven that flow into your life with the Lord
Judgment for you to be happy with yourself in him.
He ministry to the church and I shall remain in his precious
Spirit that hung out in my season of paradise in the vineyard and
One day I shall sure to proceed to be faithful in my heart with the
Image of the Lord miracle that came into my life his blessing that
Rose out of the dust of time in the season of a testimony that I shall
Stand up in his spoken word of wisdom when I receiver him hand in
My spirit of peace

16

MY LIFE HAS GROWN STRONG IN TIME OF A TINY MOMENT THAT CAME

My way for a long time in God holiness of the church in the
Vineyard for me to enjoy my life with my family and friends in a
Perfect way for my life to increase in the power of love and his
Blessing when the sheep came into the holy spirit with pray for
Everyone to his glory in the Rose Garden full of wisdom when you
Service him in the church when your soul is burning in his praise
Offering with a little victory of grace that he had for you
Branch put forth her gospel hymn in the open air of paradise
So the angels could heard her soft voice of glory in the church
With the congregation in pray and a peace offering.
A little dove came to her among the white Liles in the field
To light up the wickedness as a innocent witness that came in
Someone heart with freedom of grace for her to be wise in the eyes
Of the Lord and throughout the holy land in holiness that are
Among the shepherd in the spirit of salvation to be carry into
A view of conceiver a short rope in a race to the end in your
Stronger faith when you reach your reward in the church of a
Store that are in your path way in your life. I shed my blood upon
The crown of prayer that came down as I suffer the pain in my
Heart when the Lord show me the way to his holy word in victory
And my labor is greater before the congregation
Tellie came and rose out the midst of the congregation with her hands
Wide open before the pastor for a moment in pray and she was standing
A round the altar when she reached out to the peoples on the street as
a witness to understand the power in their heart with a little word of hope
for them to come to the Lord in the time of judgment that came into they
path of righteousness
The world of peace came into my life with the Lord glory to increased

17

MY FAITH IN HIM WITH MY TESTIMONY IN WORSHIP AS HE TOOK MY DREAM

to the Holy Land of a tiny moment of joy for me to be happy in mind
Life when I March toward that golden line on the battle field to speak
To the shepherd whom was looking for the stronger power among the
Saints in the church with their faith in the holy praise and the witness
For the Lord powerful hand that hold them in the church of worship their
To perform a dance in victory.
Bay came into his season of the glory for him to view his call in pray
Line of wisdom and my labor are not among the wicked soul whom is
Lost out there in the world with Satan but the Lord came for them in
His precious blood of paradise
I fled to the church in the vineyard my season are to worship the holy
Spirit in faith with the angels in the vineyard and Lai pitched a ideal to
Her pastor because she was open to been herself and she wanted to
Ministry to the children of the church with her heart because her life
Was not a piece of meat for the wickedness in Satan power and my life
Are in the shadow of the Lord judgment of pray and now I am learned
How to be happy again in the spirit and her bright up by his holy power
That came over the sea of glory in the season of wisdom to be took up
The word in her life to come a child of the Lord in faith as she labored by
The Holy Ghost that came upon a rock of her salvation in the church
When she receiver a increase in the ministry when the angels rose a cross
The road in righteousness of pray and the wild side of her life was full
Of grace in the season of glory when the congregation sing a hymn
That rose upon a stone. Their fled to the prayer line to pray for in the
Laid of hands
Tellie have a dream on the road upon a journey that cross the meekness
To take her to the end of holiness when the little children perform they
Play in the season of the church

33

18

THE PASTOR WAS AMAZE BY THEIR LITTLE FACE IN THE MOMENT IN PARADISE

Jet labor came down the cross by your praise in her heart for a blessing
Upon a vine that run around the wilderness that she filled a vessel of
power in the air in with a soft place of salvation in peace to the
congregation in judgment of working before the pastor On the cross
with a tiny miracle
Bay told the pastor of the church, he was blessing with a new joy on
Monday morning and he would be travel some of time on Sunday
And he join a church the next month when he came back into town
And was baptized in the gospel to worship because of his spirit was a
Very strong grace in God victory of the Holy Ghost after two years
He came a deacon in the church and the Lord remind him to be a
powerful
Shepherd in his heart for him
His life became precious in the eye of the church and he work very hard
With his faith for the Lord
That afternoon It start to rain very heavy in the city of Paradise
Some of them stay at the church until the rain stop before they
Went home
Jay Zip have a little blessing from with the power of the Lord to become
A minister of music and he have a strong in his holy spirit of the church
When he was talk to the pastor about his life in Sunday school with his
Passion of holiness that follow in his father footstep of wisdom with
His minister in the church and a angel came down in the spirit of
Victory for the shepherd who was stand around him by the power
In his life as they went fore in the command of the judgment with a
Blessing the church in your spirit of grace
Rev Lower spoken to him about the power of music in his heart along
With the rule from holy father in heaven that congregation sing a little

Hymn in victory and according to the voice of pray that rise up in the air
Of salvation and your season are a word to circle around
The world in peace that are in your heart and the saints
Fall from heaven in a blessing of grace
The little children went out to play in the vineyard of
       Holiness
Rev Zip hear the pastor word as he talked to him in
The prayer line of freedom because his voice was very
Powerful in the Lord ministry when he singer in the holy
Spirit and he have a little issue with his voice that could
Raise the dead soul in the church with a powerful hymn
In the Lord victory and according to the congregation and
He was called in the season to singer for the glory in his life
For the Lord and the mother of the church because she
Took him under her wing in the vineyard of prayer One
Sunday morning I roses up by the faith in my heart for the
Lord and he have a season for the world to see their trouble
That the lord spirit shine around me in the wilderness of
Peace was a blessing in the heart of them in happiness in the
Grace of pray Ray Zip gather some of the children in the church
To singer a hymn for the congregation
Gigi hear their voice in the vineyard of paradise when the season
Was a shine star of stone to shine all around their little souls in
The Lord season with the pastor in wisdom because he reminded
Them to stay on the right path with the Lord.
Perhaps the opportunity that shall come knock on their heart
For them in this season of grace as they go forward in the spirit
When the season of righteousness are receiver by the victory for
The lord mercy in your life that you hold with happiness in your
Ministry Of faith that come near to you
When you turn around and look in heaven with the heart
That are in your season of time for the Lord to come into
Your life with his love for you to become a precious soul
       Of his
Jet show up in the spirit of salvation when a prophet

Spoken to her heart in the holy season that came up in the
Dust of a tiny moment for her to bear the cross in her called
That burn in her soul when the Lord rose up in the spirit for a
Witness to answer God for her that came out of the wind
of holiness as a blessing to her in his love flow down into the
plan that the Lord have for her in his victory of calling and he
gather his shepherd together in the meekness of his season to
hear a soft voice in the vineyard as she went out in the gospel
to preacher a word to the peoples all around the Holy City
Of Blessing
A small child came to her with her arm open wide for hug because
The child parent was killed by a drunk driving two month ago.
Branch was unhappy living with her mother sister and she was
Six years old and her friend Molly just start the first grade to.
Their attendant the same school and Branch mother take Molly
Into her heart after 1 year Molly was happy with her aunt
Grace. Reed went to living with a friend of the family
The two children were very happy in their life and the season
Of happiness came together in their life and their visit one other
Every other weekend. MRS Risen influence them to be happy
In school. Their stay in touch with one other and due high
School and they went to church every Sunday with their two
Aunts whom living about two miles apart
Bay went into army and little sister became a preacher in the
Spirit Church with the Lord salvation
Meekness was in their season of holiness in their heart
With a moment of joy that fill they life with happiness

19

RISE UP BY THE PRECIOUS POWER

The unquenchable fire burn in my heart to change my soul
Mark talk with Rev Sea about the Sunday school after service
He was blessing by the lesson and the spirit are flow around
His soul by the word in wisdom to living by faith that came
Down out of the air. Ready was stood beside the open door
Of the church when the congregation was closing the service
Of grace in the holy word upon the wall of your heart with
God praise offering
His little nephew went out and pray to the pure spirit in his
Heart and Rev Sea was recovered by the power in the church
With the congregation as they went out of the door of the
Church with the praise dances of salvation. jay was retired
From Told Vineyard where work for forty years after that he serve
In the church as a minister of music and he was reward with a
Golden cross in peace from heaven and when someone shout
For the pastor to show them the way toward the holy town
Of Victory for a little moment in happiness that came into his life
A blessing that came into someone holy hand with a peace offering
That came out of the midst of their soul when their praise the
Church on Sunday morning in a miracle of pray.
Jet went out in a happy moment of joy for her mother Basis
Jump up in the spirit of holiness when the guest choir singing
A hymn of glory for her to connection to the new church in
Her life. My faith I can't fail in my love for the living God power
Came for me to worship him in the Holy Spirit
When he came and blessing me by the wisdom in my soul went
Out as I went out into the world with a moment in peace and
Some time I might need a little word from the Lord when I feel
Down he came and left up in his precious hand of his salvation

I will not stop praise his holy name in my life because 'he is a part
Of my heart as I look for his salvation in the middle of my soul for
Him to show me his faith in the choice word of time in the delivered
I shall chill in time of his holiness and one day I shall be the first to
Touch heaven with a little smile of joy in love for the Lord and
Nobody can compare me to someone in the church with peace
I pray in my mood of time because my victory is a part of life in
The church
Jet had appointment with the pastor of the church when she lost
Her battle to cancer in the vineyard of grace due to her ill after her
Funeral. Sea moved from Each Town and moved to a other town
Called Rock and MR Ship start to enjoy a new life in the city Jet little
Sister Page came into Holly City of class to be anoint in the spirit of
The Holy Ghost
Her mother was a pastor of a church in Each Town. Sea want to travel
So she travel for three years and after that she move back home and
Went to college.
MRS Annie has proclaim in her faith of God and her word was among
The among your daily pray in her life because she mourned for her
Daughter every day Every little moment making her life little easy
day by day as time went on in her life and she lie in the Lord faith
of wisdom
Silver have dwell in the field of unspeakable praise that
Full her life with a commandment in love for the temple
Of her praise to come out of her life and the month went
By fast in the holy shepherd that stand on the battle stone
Of heaven
Sky have a voice to be hear in the wind of the moment with
Her faith for the Lord salvation and she in close the garden
That flow into a tiny place with a little flock of birds that fly
In the air and the holy angels. Because the Lord sent them
Out of heaven to visit the innocent soul in the spirit of wisdom
In a dream with your faith and her sister came into the grace
Of love for her to go in the church with the family.
She got up and got dress for church, peace filled the air for a

Moment in the congregation with pray from the pastor and
She stood up to join the minister in faith
Ward came into her heart with his big smile to warm her soul
In peace so she could be happy again in her life with a moment
Of holiness and their journey across the city with a heavy voice
From heaven on the battle field of salvation when the Lord laid
His holy hand on the lost soul in the world so they could see
Their way to the church and his power are very deep of mine
Prayer in the open air that I have for understanding the faith
That came down in the vessel of the freedom in paradise of glory
To open up the air in your month with his victory for the world
And I stood in the flood of time to see all the faces against the
Wicked spirit in freedom and one day I shall feel free to see the
Love in my soul that all the one to be hold left behind for me
By the power for the Lord forgiving of my sin in holiness I am not
Afraid to love again now I can open my heart to the world again
And my heart is with you all and the Lord are walking with me every
Day when I praise my life in him to be a blessing by his faith in my life
As I feel for you all in the spirit of my heart every day
Sunny came in the power of meekness that rose up out the pray of
Holiness in the secret side of a tiny banquet that came in the shadow
Of innocent praise that rose out of your heart into a vessel of wisdom
For me to dance by his holy spirit in the treatment of the kingdom I
Shall stand under the foot step of the Lord in his shadow of freedom
That fall into a tiny vessel of my eye are open to the spirit to obey the
My word of the gospel to recover my life for a moment to be hear of a
Praise in the Lord honor to the church with a record to the heart for
Everyone
Gigi went up to the top of a great mountain of happiness in every
Manner of power so the church can be a stock in peace for a seed
In her life as the pastor speak to the shepherd in faith before his
Congregation to storage up her power in the judgment of peace
Because she were about to withdrawn her spirit back from the
Church so she went to the Lord in pray and he begin to work in
Her life and the shepherd on the battle field of worship for her to

Become faithful in his service of the church and she March toward
The plan that the Lord have for her. The power was strong in the
Victory with a tiny word that came down out of the air with the
Angels to watch over the world in peace because my gospel can be
Preacher to your soul every day at you left up my miracle in your
Heart and I shall judge you in my deliverer of glory in a moment
Of joy that went up into the Lord precious hands of wisdom every
Morning for you to praise him in the midst of holiness
Silver was very sad because her father have die two hours earlier
She went to the church next Sunday she was at Sunday when the
News came to her and her sister Canny came from the hospital cry
Because their father was in a car accident and died
After everything was over the two sister start two singing together
For the grace of the Lord and their travel all over the country and
Their mother pass five years earlier from cancer and one night after
Performance their have to rush Canny to the emergency room because
She have become very sick and the doctor came to the room to speak
To her about her ill and stay in the hospital for two weeks Dr Key run
Blood test on her and blood work came back, Dr Key found out she
Have the same kind cancer her mother had and when she went home
From hospital she rest for four months and after that she start to travel
With Silver was singing again and her spirit that came into the spirit
Of the Lord
Silver was happy again and little sister to travel and singing with her
Up and down the dangerous highway
To service the Lord in their life and singing for his praise in glory
Canny had to have a check up every year for cancer and the
Spirit spoken to her heart in a moment from the Lord when he
Came to her in a dream one day indeed a tiny voice came into
The spirit of wisdom to test her faith in a strong way and she obey
The will in a blessing of meekness so the church was a tool of power
In the air for her to be heal with the Lord Salvation in Canny soul
One day went out to visit with a dear friend of her in the hospital
Hero was very happy to see her and their visit along time after three
Day he went home from hospital and he call her to talk with her

About the church on Sunday and he met her because he was thank
About the joining the church it was six months since he went home
And went to church with her the next Sunday morning it was one year
Ago when Canny fine out she has cancer and it was time her
Check up and Hero went with her to the doctor for the visit
Because Silver had to work
Hero answered the called in the church in his minister of dance
For the Lord and he begin to perform in the holy spirit of
Wisdom and the pastor honor him by the power of holiness in
The Lord bring his angels into the church with a little word in
Their heart and his life are love by the congregation in the spirit
Of grace to fill the pray in the world. Hero cousin came from a
Visit and Tillie was a major part of his life by the power in God
Kingdom with the shepherd standing in the middle of the
Vineyard and plan a play in the church. The pastor entered
The holy spirit of praise for the saints of a disciple. The Holiness
Grace Church was preparing for a peace offering upon a frame of
Support in service to order the praise tribe that was scattered
In the center of someone heart with a tiny moment of learned
A few things in the church that enter your judgment with
Power for the grace of the Lord that came out of the air with a
Piece of your soul.
Sunny made a vow to praise the Lord in pray before the major
Part of the word that was in the pure air of happiness to come
Out of your mouth for you to shout to the world that your life
Are in the Lord powerful hand of righteousness in peace that
Came upon his throne with his ministry of love in the service
Of freedom
Ward came in the flesh of the Lord tear that was a major part
Of his wisdom for him to provided in the church with his ministry
Of boldness with faith as he walk before the Lord throne of
Happiness in a moment of pray that came out of the wind in time
Of for the world to see his blessing in the precious air of
Holiness someday joy shall show up in your heart and the
Rain came down on a dove wing in the Lord precious

air and one night I hear a tiny voice speak to you
In the holy spirit for me to come forward out of the shadow
And have peace with him in my life for the congregation
In peace for me to love in a blessing that cover me in the
Lord faith of praise that came with his shepherds by the
Power in my heart for the church. I shall not rush in the wind
Of a vessel in salvation of victory that fall from heaven
With the mean in his ministry to come up from the wilderness
Of his freedom
Shy met Gigi at church with the little angels that was stand
Around a big tree of holy power that dwell in the pastor soul as
He prays for them in the choose moment of paradise because she
Was happy to see her friend again because she went to visit with
Her aunt for the summer and after church their have a good
Moment playing and running with one other in connection to the
Church in salvation Sky was ten years old
Tillie have the answered to the Lord voice by the power in her
Heart as she went into the worship service and spoken to the
Children on the battle field Of grace and one Sunday morning
The pastor came to her with his hand reach to her because her
Soul was very heavy in the spirit of wisdom and the pastor came
To her in the name of the Lord and he said to her you need be
Happy so you can at peace again wit yourself
I shall stand on the word in the Lord holy name at his degrees in
My life in pray to the shepherd in the church of victory in the
Center of my heart with a piece of happiness that belong to
The Lord is in the power that flow a cross the open field in
The glory of paradise the world is the shadow in the wilderness
Of holiness and the Lord lighted up my path toward the holy land
For me to receiver my called by his precious power in my life
One day I shall stand in the holy spirit of his victory and the shadow
Came into the open air of recover of my grace in the Lord power in
His holy bible and in the sight of a miracle that re in the church and
In the wisdom due to me and mind pray that are under the shadow of
One degree that is a part of the Lord free in the war of paradise

As you journey on the battle the land for the to see your glory in
Zion
Peace is for everybody that stand on the dry land to recover with
Life that cried out to the saints in the holy city of Bethlehem
In heaven with a moment of my salvation when I walk across the
Dry up city of a voice are not hear in the Lord answered in your life
When I walk on the battle land of grace and the message came into
Someone soul with a bleed soul that is strong in your religion in a
Verse for your precious bible and I weep for a little while for the law
In the church with pray to become hold in the present of God
One day I shall dance around the Elm tree in order is among the
Peace offering in Zion
Hero rise up in the open door of freedom when the shepherds came
Into the light of glory that shine in the midst of the Holy Land of pray
My life is cover up when I turn again Satan and I meet with the
Lord one day in heaven when I enter into the Holy Ghost spirit of
Joy .The Lord view my life and his foundation are for me to come
Out of his wick world and turn my life around and me to see him
In my soul when I walk into the temple with peace and the honor
Due to his mountain in Zion with difference look into my heart for his
Love as a witness to someone in the spirit as I rise up in
His holy spirit. I have a little place to worship with the Lord
That he set before me by the power of his wisdom for me
To proceed in the presence moment of his salvation that
Enter the open air
Sunny creep into the open door of a defile time as the pastor
Preacher in a good way to his congregation with a joy that rain
Down from heaven with a pure word of happiness for them to be
Free with the Lord victory every day in their life in a billion piece of
Love that shall come into your heart with his pray of holiness that
Enter your praise moment in victory of your heart with a clean
Spirit for you to discover the plan in your soul that the Lord have
For your life in him. My life l lying in the balance line of faith
Silver have to place her unclean spirit into the honor rank to search
The understanding of her heart in the Lord beauty word of wisdom

That came into her precious life with the shepherd out there on the
Battle field in peace for her to proceed in righteousness I was very
Grateful to the pastor for a powerful word because it is a blessing in
My soul this morning and the issue in my life for me to deal with his
Word help me to face it with a moment of happiness that full my soul
In time to open the door of a best life in the church and I feel free in
Time of righteousness.
Jet have a new clean path to follow in the religion that burn like a tiny
Wild fire among the church in Zion of her soul
Some time I feel like have a little talk with the Lord I pray for peace to
Come into my heart when I endue the knowledge in the vanish power
That I heard a sound of a cymbal playing in the midst of my soul that
Follow me in the spirit of victory that came dance around heaven in
Salvation
    Hero turn around to see who was behind him. His friend
Was talk with Silver about church music in their life because the
Lord provide her with a strong voice in they soul the Lord cover him in
His spirit with his precious faith
The flame of glory came before the congregation in a hymn of cunning
Power of the Holy Ghost he was very happy that he ran into his friend
On the way out of the church park lot. Them went to Sunny house to
Visit and Sunny mother have dinner really for them because he has
Called her on his way home and. His friend was very happy to meet
MRS Ross play for her church in Paradise
Their form a gospel band of charity in the Freedom of praise for the
Little children so they can believe in their life to become strong in they
Heart for the Lord faith. The love was everlasting clock of time for them
To hold in their heart as they grown up by the time of paradise
Hero and Tellie was the singing of the group and their arrangement the
Music.
MRS Ross believe in the lesson in praise that cast a shining light into
The church with her life among the choir of the spirit in your life as
You walk toward the vineyard in the Lord grace. I wanted turn my back
On God. Their watch the clock for the time their spent together that
Afternoon. Three hours went by so fast

Cole was born to a girl name Tory who praise the love of God in the Holy City of Realized I praise my time in church of Salvation as a member

Of a little choir in the Holy City with my mother for a victory moment in Happiness in my life. Sometime my voice have a tiny strength of coaster That follow behind me in the root of my soul when I enter into a holy spirit With the tenser heart in heaven when Jesus healed my broken life with his

Faith in me

The Lord help me support my dried pain in side of my life when the Grief came into the back door of life for someone who are cry In the spirit of holiness. My pain came creep in the way for everyone To be healed by the Lord power in pray some time you feel the lost In your heart that are the benefit in happiness may you smile with Wisdom that come up in your calling of victory that are the simple Blessing of swallowed down you're your dream in the church of Faith that I walk through the door of salvation I allow the Lord to hold Me close to him with a miracle in pray under my praise tongue that Came up to the word of judgment in their soul

Proverb 14 (8) KJV The wisdom of the prudent is to understand his way but the folly of fools is deceit

20

AMY HOLINESS

The innocent blood went upon the altar with a holy
Spirit in Amy heart when she rose up on a hill in the
Holy land of Peace when her mother was in a trance
Bob came to the Holy City to be strong with his family
Who he hasn't seen in a long time because he was on
The road to find the meaning of Christmas because he
So sad and unhappy
Coffee was Bob little brother in the holiness of peace
That fill their life with a little moment in faith with
Came upon the cross in a location of wisdom
Their parents dwell in the Righteousness City of faith
With a song in the town of Christmas. Judy came out
To meet with the shepherds in the spirit of wisdom to be
A blessing by them in the holy power in her soul
Bob was on him way to the church in Grace Town of
Holiness so he could find the meaning of Christmas in
                His heart
A flood came into the Holy Town of Christmas to light up
The holy tree in the land of Peace to dry up the wet town
For someone heart and Judy stuff the little children bag with
A gift in the presence of the shepherd in the holy land of Pray
In Christmas Praise of faith that came out of their heart
Rejoice in the joyful sound that ring out in the precious time
                Of holiness
Amy were a witness before the worship power in singing to
The poor last soul for the gift in the Holy Land of Peace to the
World for a blessing in someone life with a Christmas wish before
The church as their pay in the Holy City with the shepherd that
Came fore to meet with Mercy Ann and Amy was close friend

For a long time when their met Scott Joy in the Little Town of
Wisdom
Scott have a older brother and his name was Paul and he would
Play his trumpet in the Holy Land of Peace in order of the
Almighty on a bright Christmas morning in a precious camp
Meeting place of gospel and in your salvation as a witness
In the glory yard of prayer for everyone to see the Christmas
Tree in the Holy Land of hope
Amy came int he church with a gift of thanksgiving for
Everyone to see the blessing of joy on Christmas morning
That the Almighty had for you in his precious peace of peace
For the world to be at the grace with holiness
Amy dance around the Christmas tree in a remember a moment
When she journeys into the court of prayer to change the holy spirit
of judgment in someone soul as you travel to a foreign city
in the unexpected spirit in the holy land
Some time you focus on the meaning of Christmas to be
Precious to you in the temple of salvation
The crime of joy is a time for your peace to come into
Your life as you journey toward the gift in Christmas miracle
For the world
I heard the trumpet playing in the holy spirit of my heart
With a sound in pray to under cover a peace offering in wisdom
With a moment in Amy heart when she March toward the Holy
Land in Bethlehem
Some time my way are dark by the power in the Holy
Land by the Almighty light in the hand of the living God
One day he came to me in the spirit when I receive the gift
Of Christmas and I will be thankful for peace in the Holy Land
With Amy standing by my side
One day I will be weeping for salvation in the temple of joy
When the shepherd came to me in the presence of the living
God as I go forth to the holy land in victory
Bob went out into the camp meeting with a friend of his who
Name was Jerry Lite to review a new play in the Holy Land of

Wisdom for a gift of a Christmas dance
A new sound came for me to be happy in my life with the shepherd
On the battle field of victory
I singing a little hymn in praise for a Christmas gift to the angels
A with blessing in peace to the temple that proceed in a foreign
Land and in order to journey into the court that they focus on the
Road to victory toward a plot of salvation with an expected friend
Was name Holly Ann and she was very happy little woman.
She went out to see the parade upon a shining star of
Heaven as a gift in the moon light of a Christmas blessing
Janet ministry to the shepherd in the foreign land with a
Moment in peace for everyone in their heart to see the
Victory of glory
Jerry and Lynn went out into a foreign land to praise the
New baby in Bethlehem
God journey with me into the valley of love and peace
For me to feel his spirit in my life as I journey with his holy
Saints that follow a bright shining star to the Holy Town in
Pray
My love and spirit were in the season for me to be happy in mind
Life with the holy baby in the promised land in pray to the world
In a little moment of thanks for a better way to show me the
Meaning of a Christmas gift to the church in praise.
Someday you make consumer your life in God gift that he has for me
To feel happy again in his precious grace in your life with Amy and
Holly
Release the list of salvation gift beyond your demand into the
Wilderness on a tour to the Holy Town in wisdom I spent some
Time in God pray of praise toward Canaan with my testimony
In glory for me to service him in my heart with the congregation
In the sanctuary
My gift as a sacrifice to the baby upon a star of Christmas miracle
Amy was talking to Holly and Janet about her life in God
My mother encourages me in the holy spirit to follow my dream
And have I all way love music until now

My mother are with the Lord and she live with dementia above
Five years some time she could fight and climbing out of the window
And some time it would be hard for us to keep her inside of the
House the door at be boat lock to keep her in with this disease
It was a hard on us and sometime we would have a rough time
With her
God reach out to me to living by his faith in my heart to hold
On to his spirit that he laid out for me in a plot of salvation for
To tell my story some day to the world if I want to his faith are
Apart of my life in the innocent power of his precious blood
In the church that came down in a word for the Lord rainbow
The congregation can swallow down the precious word of
Wisdom and there are go into the green sea
I shall understanding the power in my testimony of heaven
And my supplication went out to reach some one heart in the
Spirit of faith
One day my praise shall come into the open air with a star to
Shine down that precious path of life in God holy blood of pray
For the world to see the miracle coming their way as they enter
Into the temple of Victory
Some day I shall rejoice in the church with a peace offering from
The Lord in heaven and his commandment are a golden moment
For me to show my faith to the world in recover of the great power
That came down the path of life that matter to the Lord in time of
Salvation and my heart can reach out to the Lord in the world
Holy pray
Some time I feel like a war are a high wall in the holy city of freedom
God have touched my soul in a shadow of his victory in mercy according
To the holy word of holiness in peace
A hand of wisdom is a thing to be continued in a blessing that endue
The shower of judgment came upon the sun of glory that in the
Whirlwind to be a blessing that answered me out of the spirit
That cover the power in Rainy life when the spirit came into a
Tiny voice of judgment that rose up in the midst of the air
I hear a soft voice in the sound according to the living God in

A blessing of praise to the Lord
My soul is in the church of knowledge with praise to come out
The darkness of hope is in my shadow of pray I shall enter
into the light of glory with the angels
some day I shall shout before the Lord in the temple and
God will open his door for me to enter into my dream in mind
life as I walk with him upon the star of life when I pray in
peace to the world
salvation is a miracle to directed me to my Christmas gift
that come out of my heart into the precious light of grace
that follow me to the tree of holiness that deliver my spirit
under the Christmas star when it shines for me to become
hold in his faith that are close to in the Christmas bell
ringing out around the world when he pours out the pray
in Bethlehem for the three wise men to follow the shining
star into the Holy City to see the new baby in your heart as
you March into the temple with your love that came down
from heaven with Rainy and Pennie
Amy went out to find the meaning of Christmas miracle to
Know the gift for a blessing in the Christmas spirit to be cast
In the pray of your faith in the power of the Lord
I consume a hymn in the Holy City of Grace for you to be at
Peace in your life
I hear a loud rejoice hymn to prepare my heart for a song
In the Holy Power City
Pattie came into Amy heart with a blessing from God because he
Had a planed for her life in him that was for to follow into his precious
Path of faith
Pattie have visit her in the spirit of wisdom because her friend had
Die in a accident two years ago they was very close friend and her
Love would lift her up when she feels sad and Pattie would show her
how
To restore her faith by the power in prayer for Amy to go forth to
Receiver a blessing in her life from out of the door of heaven
God are with Amy every moment as she walks in his shadow one day

She shall be strong in the faith of God
My love shall dwell in a part of my soul of God everlasting prayer
In the Holy City of salvation Pattie love flows into my heart with
Grace and when I stand up in the pure power of righteousness for a
Blessing that enter into my heart Amy receiver a little package
From Pattie mother Allie. Amy was very happy to receiver the
Gift three day before Christmas and she put the gift under the
Tree with all the other gifts
Holly choose a precious offering to the people of her gift to
Bethlehem when her spirit shows up in the temple she jump
For joy to see the little holy baby in the spirit of holiness so she
Can behold the power in dancing for the temple to rejoice and to
Spread out her life in the Holy City with the shepherds in the
Wilderness
Amy have a measuring cup of pure oil to wash her soul with and
She answered the voice of the Lord in her heart when he called
Her in the spirit and she was very happy to heard from heaven and
When the shepherd call to her out of the blue wind of time for Amy
Have a little gift for Jesus in Bethlehem
Her little brother Judah came to meet her at the mall with some
Good news that a friend of her was looking for her . Ray came
Home for a short visit because he was in the army and he left
A Christmas gift for her
She was very happy to hear from him and he was away for three
Years because their was very close before he went into the army
Amy have a big smile on her face as she enters into the Holy City of
Bethlehem when she ran into Ray they hug one other and they had
A good time laughing and having fun with one other
The mall was a mad house of shopping and they enjoyed the time
They spend with one other Amy and Judah because everything was
At peace with them
Judah met Sai in the Praying Town of Wisdom to finish his Christmas
Shopping. Sai was very close to his family for about ten years
Holly did lift up Amy soul in the prayer with the holy angel's that
Stand under the shadow of the living God in the wind of praise

That came up in the air
The Christmas season was a peaceful time in all of their life with
The living God when I feel the precious spirit under the shadow
In Bethlehem
I shall praise the Christmas victory in my heart that are in the
temple with the shepherds that are in the wilderness of grace
that follow them toward the Holy City of love by the power with
the host that came down for a spoken word in faith of a hymn in
glory
God have a path way for you to follow him toward his kingdom to
Enjoyed his angels in Bethlehem for you to stand under the
Christmas tree that light up their way to the Holy City.
A service of golden a moment in time of a Christmas blessing
In someone life when I show up in the open spirit of glory as I
March toward the Holy City of wisdom in a powerful
Answered in my life said Amy to her friend Holly
God was holding a cup of his holy oil in his hand for all of
His shepherds in Bethlehem with faith for you to become
Holy by his power in the wind of time and in the temple
For a Christmas blessing under the tree of holiness for you
To shout in peace of wisdom
My soul shall dwell in present of the Lord due to the
Shining moon in the command of your supplication in the
Kingdom of heaven with a helping judgment in the white
Path of faith in your shadow of praise to you in the living
God moment
When I tell my story in the wind of grace according to my heart
Of time in God freedom and he will show me the way to his
Home someday down the road of his salvation that I shall follow
Him to the temple in peace and I shall cry out to the angels
In Holy City that impact my testimony in the mercy prayer of
Love
Holly and Amy was talked about they plan for the Christmas
Holiday as they went into the store to shopping for gifts for they
Love ones.

Amy turn around and saw Ray and his friend shopping in the
Mall too and her heart start to skipped like a wild fire burning
In side of her life
When they eyes lock together in the open spirit of under standing
Power that rose up in her voice of peace as she said hello again
Ray have fall in love with her but she don't know that he was crazy
About her and he told her he was in love with her and right after the
Christmas holiday they were marry two years late and move to the
Town of Salvation
Judah stay behind in Holy City because he had a high
Paid job and he loves the city of Holiness
Inclined my life with the shepherd of Bethlehem that
Endured to all the power in love in my heart for my sister
And her husband Bob was very happy at last because he
Finally found the meaning of Christmas and when he went
To the temple of grace and he went into the holiday season
With his family and friend as their stand around the Christmas
Tree to celebrate the holiday with a gift of holiness in a word
Of faith that came down from heaven
They enjoyed the holiday with the full life of wisdom
The mall was very business that day after Christmas
Amy and Judah were at peace at last.

Printed in the United States
By Bookmasters